FINISHING LINE PRESS

www.finishinglinepress.com

Slippery Surfaces

poems by

Donna Spruijt-Metz

Finishing Line Press
Georgetown, Kentucky

Slippery Surfaces

ACKNOWLEDGMENTS

With many thanks to the editors of the following journals, wherein these
poems appeared, sometimes in different form:

Poetry Northwest: The New Science of Slippery Surfaces
Juked: School Me
Ellis Review: 1960—Star of David charm tucked in

I am deeply grateful to my poetry teachers and mentors—Guy Bennett,
Dennis Phillips, Paul Vangelisti, Alan Shapiro, Afaa Michael Weaver, Karin
Gottshall, Rick Barot, Wayne Miller, Gabrielle Calvocoressi, Maggie Smith,
and Sarah Manguso. You opened me up along the way.

I have been blessed with a fine community of writers and poets who have
spent so much time talking about writing with me, reading each other's work
or writing with each other over several years of our Daily Grind group, Darcy
Vebber, Roy White, Crystal Stone, Allison Albioni, Meghan Dunn, Keith
Wilson, Annette Wong, Michelle Peñaloza, Annie Reid, Monét Cooper, Laura
Hogan and Nan Cohen.

Thank you Gershom, my husband, who supported and encouraged me
through my restlessness and career changes, and you, my daughter Mishala
Bateman, and your husband Chris, for your inspiration and wry humor.

Publisher: Leah Maines
Editor: Christen Kincaid
Cover Art: Gershom, Gershom-art.com
Author Photo: Tami Bahat
Cover Design: Leah Huete

Printed in the USA on acid-free paper.
Order online: www.finishinglinepress.com
                also available on amazon.com

Author inquiries and mail orders:
Finishing Line Press
P. O. Box 1626
Georgetown, Kentucky 40324
U. S. A.

Table of Contents

1.

Ponytail

Remember Patti Playpal?
Dolls the size of a six-year-old girl?
She could be hard to carry
when running to catch the plane,
but I gripped her by the ponytail
while my mother gripped me,
her left hand dragging me through
the terminal. In her other hand,
white three-quarter gloves,
red leather handbag.
Did you know, before jets
the flight from Los Angeles
to Honolulu took ten hours?
If your father had just died
you got a pull-down bed.
The stewardess pulled it down
made it up for us nicely
but there was hardly room
for the two of us.

Water Skis

The girl on the sand
sits a safe way back,
only her own hand
to shield her
from the insistent sun,
eyes fixed on her mother
far from shore,
olive-skinned,
vainglorious,
swooping back
and forth expertly
across the boat's wake.

To Forgiveness

I hated you
even then—for
the sandy cups of
tepid milk on
the beach in
my vagina the terrible
sand—your skin

so olive mine
red red
like the blood
that came too
late, an off-season plum
from the twisted

tree—I hated you for
lying—for your own
stubborn truth
you stored—
a pebble under

your tongue
but then you
sang sang
at the piano
—the men
at the parties
winding them
all around your
pretty pretty—

you only spoke
to me too
late by then
under my
tongue a warrior's

whip that drew
red red
welts into your

shattering
mind oh please
I left you
on the streets of
New York—my husband
complaining of your slow
gait my child just

wanting your
love—to be
seen—and I
remembered wanting
that the dull ache of
desire I still
mistake for
love—but
you had your
bitter pebble

I could not
remove it not with
the plyers of
prayer—which you
rejected—take those
candles away—not the
knives of
achievement—never
quite oh please even
bless me father
dead dead dead dead—

not even
with that
the pebble—it was
all you had
turns out
you thought
it was all
you had

I placed you
in the best of
them good food—
sushi on Wednesdays
ice cream on Sundays—
beach and sand
on the horizon
from your window
a kind caregiver
a phone that you
could no longer
use.

1960—Star of David charm tucked in

I get caught shoplifting
at the dime store. Even though we
are the outsiders, they
call my mother.   Tommy calls

me a kike on Halloween. The other kids,
ghouls and ghosts, bop girls and real bad
Elvis impersonators,   they stand there
in silence, sharp like glass,
the devil's pact,
the irreversible stepping over
to muteness,

me, on the porch with the
manicured bonsai, dressed
as Queen Esther with an   empty bag.
I shrink back

indoors like Saran Wrap exposed
to flames or Wonder Bread in a
child's vicious hands.   My father,
he built all their magnificent
waterfront homes.   We Jews
just aren't allowed
to live in them.

My mother
thought she could   hide
this from me.

Dendrochronology for My Mother

This ring tells of fine wild sex
and these of music.

Narrow as a witch hunt
ill-omened as a name,
these tell of age—
low-slung breasts,
incontinence, slow gait,
your ruined face.

Or these—
they record the many veils
that crept over clocks
and mirrors, the patient
pitchers of water

And what of these,
the ones that tell
of your obstinate heart,
and the six-winged spirits
that sealed your mouth with coals.

Daughter and Mother, Amsterdam, Tram 4

Stadhouderskade

Frederiksplein
Did you ever miss him?

Prinsengracht
    No, I was too angry.

Keizersgracht

Rembrandtplein

Spui
How did he really die?

Dam

Centraal Station

Dam

Cold War

Pale and wall-eyed, the child waits.
She's got corrective shoes,
a birthday party,
clowns and magicians,
hot sun on the patio,
cruel friends. She's got a father
who makes a late entrance
with an imposing toy car.
Deep inside the cool house, her mother
plays the piano. There is ice
in crystal tumblers.

Under the Piano

So small, I can slip
from hallway to living room
through the sliding

pinewood door
and crawl unnoticed
under the black

grand piano. Mother
plays for the party.
She sings,

beautiful in her red dress.
Large diamonds
rest on a plate

with half-eaten crackers,
rings too heavy
for playing.

Father's hidden
bar by the bookshelf
mounted on piano hinges

is open. Everyone drinks.

My Daughter's Shampoo

is open on
the shower floor.
She has washed her hair,
gone to work.

I still feel the first
weight of her, still
remember her
upside-down

on the monkey bars,
hair hanging down,
dress hanging down,
first veil.

Daughter and Mother, Amsterdam, Tram 4

Spui
> *But you know, I've told you.*

Rembrandtplein
How did he die?

Keizersgracht
> *Once I surprised him at his office in the city.*

Prinsengracht
Go on.

Frederiksplein
> *We went with a group to his favorite city restaurant.*

Stadhouderskade

Ceintuurbaan
> *The Maître D' greeted him: "Where is your wife tonight?"*

Lutmastraat

Amstelkade
> *A few days later, I told him I wanted a divorce.*

Victorieplein
> *Looking back it seems odd, but we had dinner that night with friends.*

Waalstraat
> *He kept saying things like: "What do you think a man should eat for his last meal?" He was always so melodramatic. And he was drinking.*

Maasstraat

Dintelstraat
Go on.

2.

Building Materials

The man of God
wanders through the stone yard
past dappled granite,

veined marble,
good black shoes
dulled and dusty,

lost in the narrow aisles,
as if there were
a synagogue

in every stone,
not only majestic
hotels and sleek bathrooms.

In the back of the yard
he finds the bricks
seared by fire,

choses them
to build the next
place of meeting.

School me
   —Psalm 25

What good is this shame?
The debt,
the deficit. It costs us
it mounts us and
it multiplies.

the only mercy
          is sloughing it off
some kind of storage, remembering
          to forget.

God, you are riddled
with caves—all the
merciful ways
of darkness

but I have
such trouble with your name

what to call you,
how to pronounce
all the many
vowels. Forgive me.
This is embarrassing.

I do choose You.
I'm listening—
could You just
reach   down to me?

Here, I made this nest, full
of half-truths, I am
learning to wait for
You. It would be good
to wait
together.

Cold Call

Needles in my back
set just so

trying to create a
singular frequency—

hear me, Lord?

Daughter and Mother, Amsterdam, Tram 4

Europaplein
> *He didn't come home that night.*

Station RAI
> *Two days later I got the phone call.*

Drentepark

Station RAI
The phone call...

Europaplein
> *Yes.*

Dintelstraat
Yes?

Maasstraat
> *That he had been found dead.*

Waalstraat
Where?

Victorieplein
> *In a hotel room. They finally found him because his fancy red Thunderbird was parked for too long in the parking lot. So they got to looking around.*

Amstelkade
So how did he die, then?

Geryon

In a dream I offer this whole world
to my father. Geryon perches
lightly, her red wings extending,

relaxing—breathing as if
they were her lungs, beating
as if they were her scorched heart,

as if wings could love
or be loved. The heart is broken,
the wings are whole, and I ask

if that's the price. I harbor a world
of singular beings within my winged body.
They live behind red doors

carved into my skin.
I don't remember the pain of their carving.
Behind each bloody door lives

a singular being with a singular story.
I listen to the complaints
of my tenants—

their petty battles,
their tales of appetites,
their feuds and bloated bowels.

I am the red land that travels.
My bloody, chiseled doors
open and close.

In a dream, I offer this whole world
to my father, but it isn't enough
to convince him to live.

The Web Teaches the Spider

Snip the web of an orb spider,
leave it dangling
and it will learn to fish—
to reel in its prey.

Animals with small
nervous systems
offload burdensome processing—

thoughts sprawl out
into the body,
into the thinking web.

Where receptors
are missing,
a part of the world ceases
to exist.

Thus, the arm knows how
to move the arm
the hand
knows how to shoot the gun.

The New Science of Slippery Surfaces

is revolutionizing containers.
Oil will slide through pipelines,
glue will flow, bacteria will be unable

to find purchase in stents and IV lines.
Through my one summer
as an incompetent waitress

I watched people trying to slap
ketchup out of bottles, then
use a knife. Here in the coffee shop,

I wait for you and watch
a student at the next table wrestle
with the Sriracha. And you,

my daughter, in your doctor's coat,
your wedding ring, sit down
across from me. I try not to want

too much. Consider all the ways
we try to get things out
that seem to want to stay in,

as if there were a will to it.

Daughter and Mother, Amsterdam, Tram 4

Lutmastraat

Ceintuurbaan
> *Well. Apparently he had taken all kinds of pills. He'd been saving up. A full bottle of antidepressants. And then drank a full bottle of liquor.*

Stadhouderskade

Frederiksplein
> *I didn't know he was depressed, or that he had been seeing a shrink.*

Prinsengracht
So he killed himself? Committed suicide?

Keizersgracht

Rembrandtplein

Spui
Did he leave, like, a note?

Dam
> *Oh yes. He left me a letter. He left you a letter.*

Central Station

Dam
What?

Spui

> *All this nonsense about how sorry he was. I ripped them up and threw them away.*

Rembrantplein

Keizersgracht

Prinsengracht

Frederiksplein

Stadhouderskade

Fifteen

My daughter is at her mirror
with eyeliner
as she touches it to her left eye...

...I am at my mirror,
my mother watching me.

My husband bought me a mirror

Travel size—5X magnification.

Texting, late at night about to sign off
he says: One more thing. he says: Your father
risked his life to fight Nazis on the beaches
of Normandy. Now it is our turn.

> my father: The man restless, fast cars,
> many women, the man who left
> to meet his death early—fist full of
> pills, belly full of liquor the man
> who took his own life, and some of mine
> with him. He made his own choice when he left—
> not my idea of a hero. I was
> a child. Now, am I a woman with a
> rusty narrative?   Screen blinks. I ask:

How? We text back and forth, art
as politics, his teaching, my research
it all seems desultory.

> —the 'fun war'—my mother entertaining
> the troops, beautiful in her uniform,
> long legged, her 'band' three beauties posing
> with uniformed men in China,
> in the South Pacific, her short snorter
> ever growing—she had a blast. She
> told her stories. As a child, and
> as young woman living in Holland
> where the Jewish population had been
> wiped out—I squirmed at those stories—
> her joyful recounting, the men, the
> countries, the airplanes but now—now I see
> she played her part.   Screen blinks, he says:

What is enough? When can you look
at yourself in the mirror? The mirror,

        a diary, a reflection. Take it—
        to the river. Submerge it in the
        water. Tilt it—can you see
        your own face?   Wash
        this face.   This mirrored face.

Donna Spruijt-Metz is a poet, translator, and Professor of Psychology and Preventive Medicine at the University of Southern California. Her first career was as a professional flutist. While working on her MFA in Flute at California Institute of the Arts, she played bass guitar in a David Bowie tribute band. She followed her teacher to the Netherlands and studied at the Royal Conservatory in Den Haag. While performing as a professional flutist, she went back to school and eventually got a PhD in Psychology and Medical Ethics from the Vrije Universiteit in Amsterdam. After 22 years in The Netherlands, she moved with her husband and daughter back to the United States. They live in L.A. with a drop-dead gorgeous Australian Shepherd. She received an MFA in Creative Writing from Otis College of Art and Design. Her work has appeared or is forthcoming in venues such as *Vinyl, The Rumpus, Occulum, the American Journal of Poetry, Naugatuck River Review, Juked* and *Poetry Northwest.*

CPSIA information can be obtained
at www.ICGtesting.com
Printed in the USA
LVHW041916190419
614903LV00001B/24/P

9 781635 348903